J 977.3 LAR 2024

Indiana

Larsen, Ib.

CARVER COUNTY LIBRARY

DISCOVERING THE UNITED STATES

Indiana

BY IB LARSEN

Kids Core
An Imprint of Abdo Publishing
abdobooks.com

abdobooks.com

Published by Abdo Publishing, a division of ABDO, PO Box 398166, Minneapolis, Minnesota 55439. Copyright © 2025 by Abdo Consulting Group, Inc. International copyrights reserved in all countries. No part of this book may be reproduced in any form without written permission from the publisher. Kids Core™ is a trademark and logo of Abdo Publishing.

Printed in the United States of America, North Mankato, Minnesota.
052024
092024

THIS BOOK CONTAINS RECYCLED MATERIALS

Cover Photo: Sean Pavone/Shutterstock Images
Interior Photos: Darron Cummings/AP Images, 4–5; Bonnie Taylor Barry/Shutterstock Images, 6 (top left); Jon Benedictus/Shutterstock Images, 6 (top right); Shutterstock Images, 6 (bottom left), 6 (bottom right), 16, 24, 26; Sports Studio Photos/Getty Images Sport/Getty Images, 7; William Reagan/Shutterstock Images, 9; Kenneth Keifer/Shutterstock Images, 10; Don Knight/The Herald-Bulletin/AP Images, 12–13; Circa Images/Glasshouse Images/Alamy, 15; Ken Wolter/Shutterstock Images, 18, 28 (Notre Dame); Pawel Gaul/iStockphoto, 20–21, 28 (Indianapolis); Jon Lauriat/Shutterstock Images, 22, 28 (Indiana Dunes); Zack Frank/Shutterstock Images, 25; Red Line Editorial, 28 (map), 29

Editor: Laura Stickney
Series Designer: Katharine Hale

Library of Congress Control Number: 2023949345

Publisher's Cataloging-in-Publication Data

Names: Larsen, Ib, author.
Title: Indiana / by Ib Larsen
Description: Minneapolis, Minnesota: Abdo Publishing, 2025 | Series: Discovering the United States | Includes online resources and index.
Identifiers: ISBN 9781098293840 (lib. bdg.) | ISBN 9798384913115 (ebook)
Subjects: LCSH: U.S. states--Juvenile literature. | Indiana--History--Juvenile literature. | Midwest States--Juvenile literature. | Physical geography--United States--Juvenile literature.
Classification: DDC 973--dc23

All population data taken from:
"Estimates of Population by Sex, Race, and Hispanic Origin: April 1, 2020 to July 1, 2022." *US Census Bureau, Population Division*, June 2023, census.gov.

CONTENTS

CHAPTER 1
The Indy 500 4

CHAPTER 2
The People of Indiana 12

CHAPTER 3
Places in Indiana 20

State Map 28
Glossary 30
Online Resources 31
Learn More 31
Index 32
About the Author 32

The Indianapolis Motor Speedway can fit around 350,000 people. In May 2023, more than 330,000 fans attended the 107th Indy 500.

CHAPTER 1

The Indy 500

It was May 30, 1911. The first Indianapolis (Indy) 500 car race was about to begin. More than 90,000 people watched as 40 cars drove up to the racetrack's starting line. The winner of the 500-mile (805 km) race would get $10,000.

Indiana Facts

DATE OF STATEHOOD
December 11, 1816

CAPITAL
Indianapolis

POPULATION
6,833,037

AREA
36,420 square miles
(94,327 sq km)

STATE BIRD
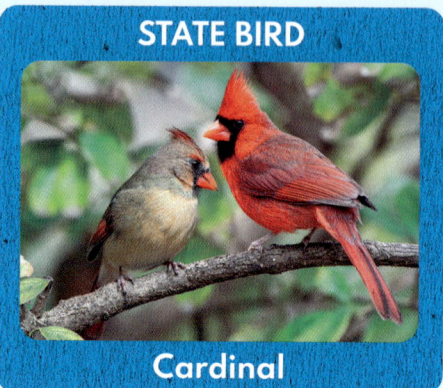
Cardinal

STATE TREE

Tulip tree

STATE FLOWER

Peony

STATE STONE
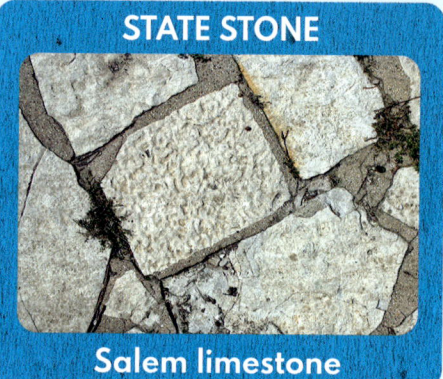
Salem limestone

Each US state has a different population, size, and capital city. States also have state symbols.

Soon, the race was on. Engines roared, tires squealed, and smoke spilled into the air. Six hours and 42 minutes later, driver Ray Harroun won the race.

6

In the 1911 Indy 500, winner Ray Harroun drove a car called the Marmon Wasp. He helped design it.

The Indy 500 takes place once a year in Indianapolis, Indiana. The drivers race at the Indianapolis Motor Speedway. The Indy 500 is one of the most famous car races in the world. People from all over the world come to watch the race.

Indiana's Land

Indiana is in the US region called the Midwest. To its north lie Michigan and Lake Michigan.

Ohio borders the state on the east. Illinois borders it on the west. South of Indiana is Kentucky.

Indiana has forests and grasslands. Its forests contain trees such as hickory, maple, oak, and tulip trees. The state is also home to many birds, including cardinals. The land in southern Indiana is hilly. But the state is mostly flat. The northern part of the state has many small lakes.

Why Is Indiana So Flat?

Indiana is one of the flattest states in the country. This is because of huge chunks of ice called glaciers. About 50,000 years ago, they moved very slowly across much of the state. This left behind the mostly flat landscape that makes up Indiana today.

More than 80 percent of Indiana's land is made up of farmland and forests.

The land in southern Indiana is very **fertile**. Farmers grow crops there.

Indiana has many lakes and rivers. The northern border of the state has a coastline on Lake Michigan. The largest lake within Indiana's borders is Monroe Lake. Important rivers include the Ohio River, the Wabash River, and the White River.

In Michigan City, Indiana, people can see a lighthouse and explore beaches along Lake Michigan.

Indiana's Climate

Indiana has four seasons. In winter, the state gets a lot of snow. The weather is hot and humid in the summer. In the spring, the state can get tornadoes and other severe storms. Sometimes cold air from the north passes over Lake Michigan. This brings extra rain and snow to the northern part of Indiana.

Explore Online

Visit the website below. What new information did you learn about Indiana that wasn't in Chapter One?

Indiana

abdocorelibrary.com/discovering-indiana

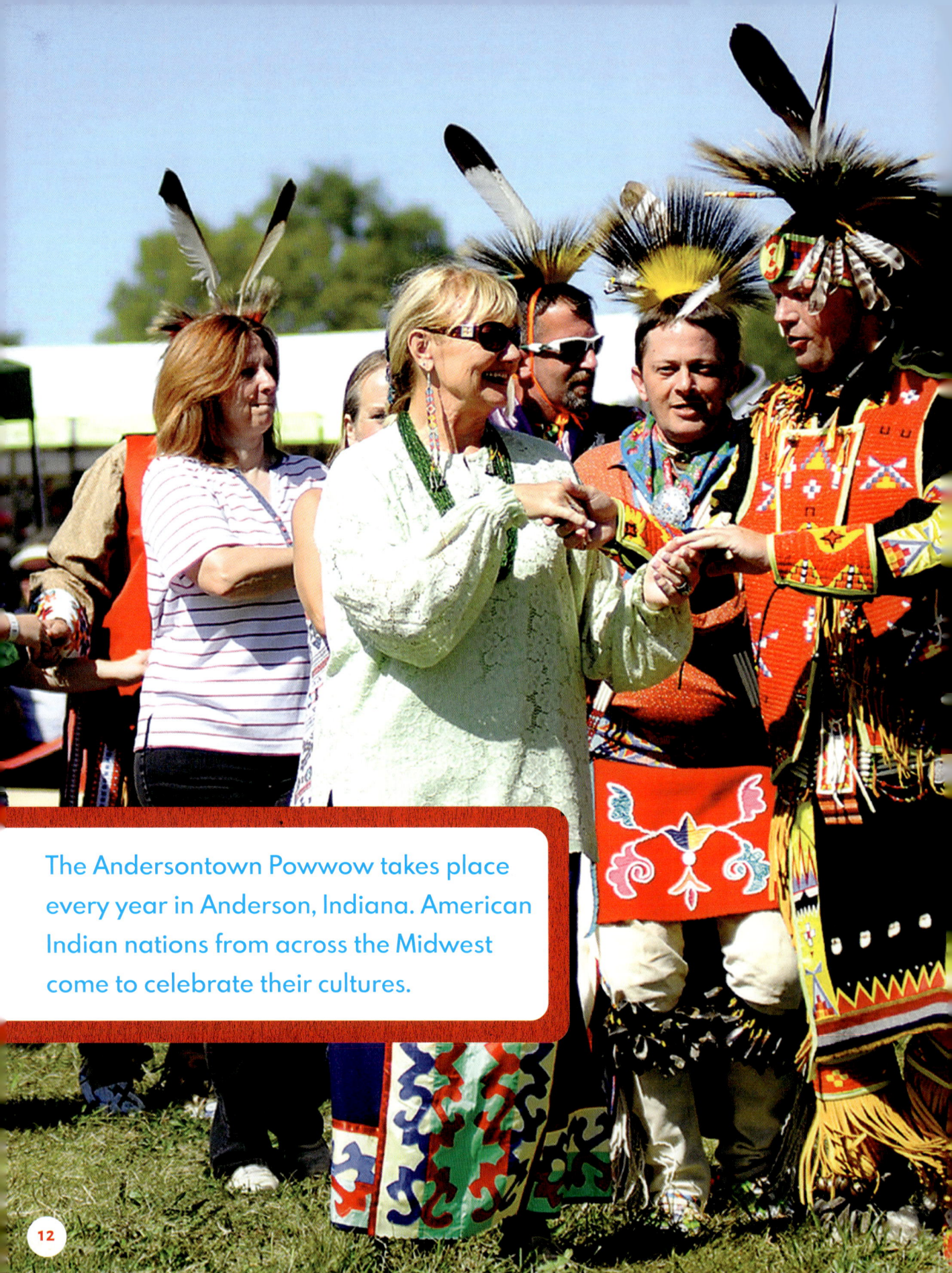

The Andersontown Powwow takes place every year in Anderson, Indiana. American Indian nations from across the Midwest come to celebrate their cultures.

CHAPTER 2

The People of Indiana

Indiana means "land of the Indians." American Indians arrived in the area about 12,000 years ago. They hunted animals and farmed crops. Over time, different cultures developed tools, weapons, and foods.

Many American Indian nations have lived in Indiana. These include the Miami, Potawatomi, and Delaware. When French and British **colonists** arrived in the area, they wanted land. They fought American Indians and each other.

The United States **acquired** the **territory**. The US government forced most American Indian nations off the land. In 2022, about 30,000 American Indians lived in Indiana.

In the 1800s, more white settlers came to Indiana. Many were from eastern states such as Virginia and North Carolina. Other **immigrants** came from Germany, Ireland, and England.

In 2022, 84 percent of people in Indiana were white. About 10 percent were Black. Eight percent were Hispanic or Latino, and

In the 1800s and 1900s, many immigrants came to Indiana cities to find jobs. Some worked in factories such as cotton mills.

3 percent were Asian. Less than 1 percent were American Indian.

Culture

Indiana is home to several unique foods.

One is sugar cream pie, or Hoosier pie.

Early Quaker and Amish settlers were likely the first to make sugar cream pie. Many people call it Indiana's unofficial state pie.

It is different from other cream pies because it does not contain eggs. The pork tenderloin sandwich is also popular. It was likely invented in Huntington, Indiana, in 1904. It features deep-fried pork loin on a hamburger bun.

Basketball is one of the most popular sports in Indiana. The Indiana Pacers are a men's professional basketball team. The Indiana Fever are a women's professional basketball team. Both teams play at Indianapolis's

Gainbridge Fieldhouse. The state's football team is called the Indianapolis Colts.

Industry

Many people in Indiana have jobs **manufacturing** products such as cars, medicine, and machines. The company Koch Enterprises manufactures chemicals and paper.

Hoosiers

People from Indiana are sometimes called Hoosiers. No one knows where this name came from. Some people believe early settlers created it. They would say the phrase "Who's here?" whenever somebody knocked on their doors.

Notre Dame is considered to be one of the best universities in Indiana. Its campus has several historic buildings, such as the golden-domed Main Building.

It employs around 120,000 people. Other people perform services, such as selling insurance. There are many farmers in Indiana too. They grow soybeans and corn.

Education is also important in Indiana. The state is home to colleges such as the University of Notre Dame and Purdue University. These universities provide many jobs for people.

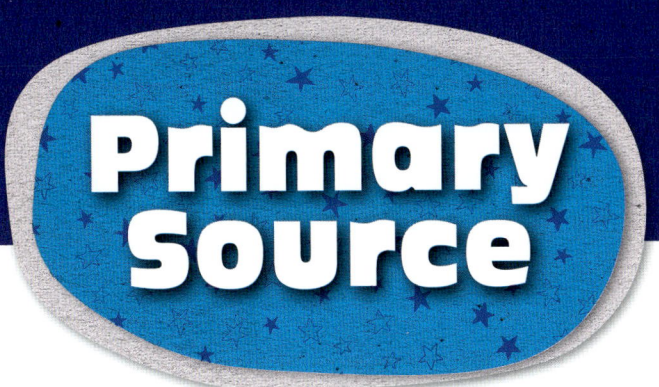

Indiana farmer Tom Murphy's favorite part of farming is watching his crops grow. He said:

> It is always a sense of accomplishment to see your hard work growing in the fields and be proud to harvest what you planted.

Source: "Interview with Valparaiso Farmer Tom Murphy." *Shirley Heinze Land Trust*, n.d., heinzetrust.org. Accessed 9 Aug. 2023.

What's the Big Idea?

Read this quote carefully. What is its main idea? Explain how the main idea is supported by details.

In the center of downtown Indianapolis is Monument Circle. This area is home to the Soldiers and Sailors Monument, *center*.

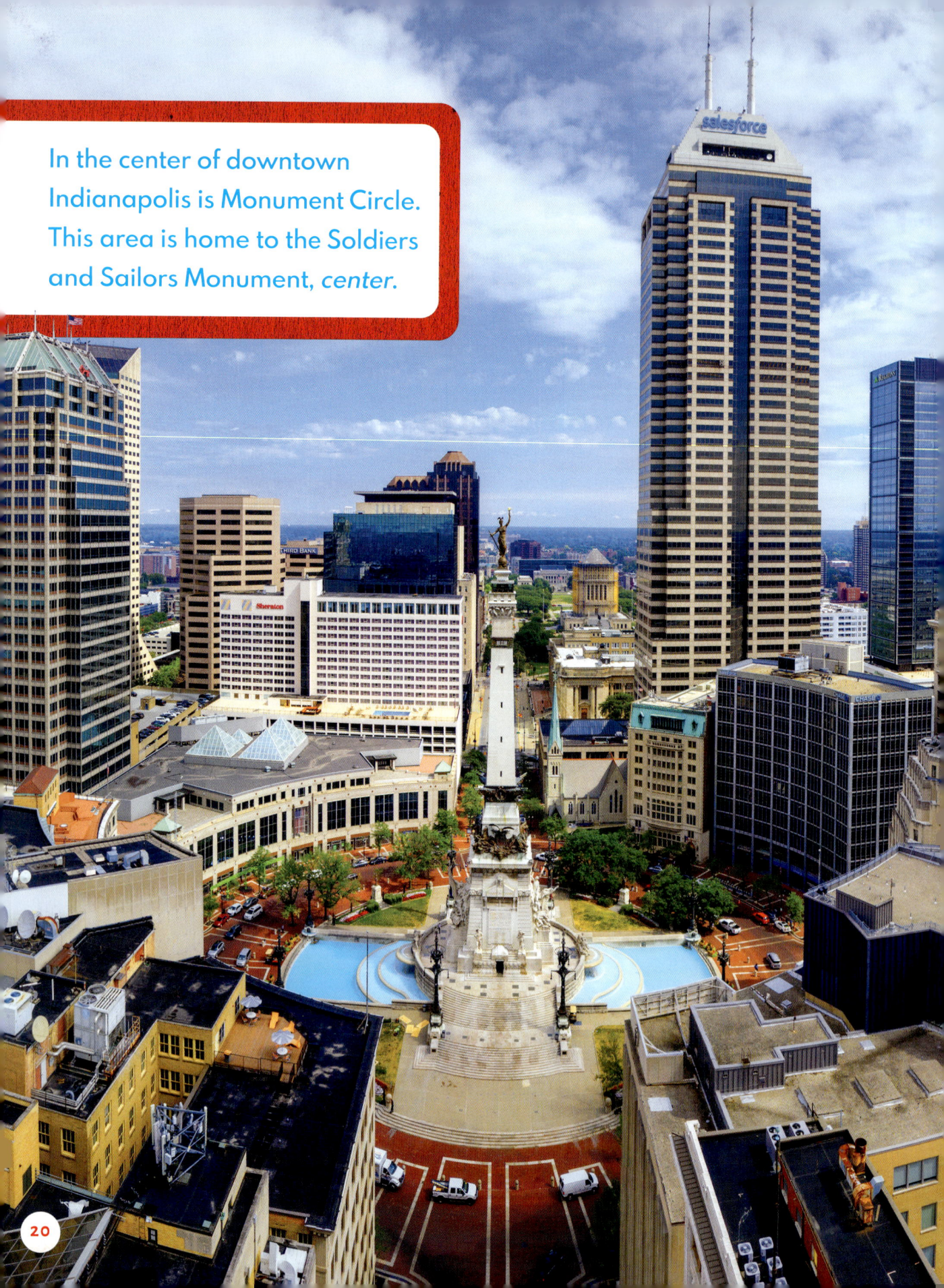

Places in Indiana

Indiana has a few big cities and many small towns. The state's capital is Indianapolis. It is located in central Indiana. Other important cities include Fort Wayne, Evansville, and South Bend.

At Indiana Dunes National Park, visitors can hike the Dune Succession Trail. It features more than 200 wooden stairs.

Parks

Indiana is home to Indiana Dunes National Park. It's named after sand dunes that run along Lake Michigan's southern shore. Visitors can hike on trails or swim in the lake. They can also learn about plants and animals in the area.

Indiana has 24 state parks. One is Chain O'Lakes State Park. Visitors can take boats out on the nine **kettle lakes**, which are connected to each other. People can also hike, camp, or bird-watch.

Mounds State Park features ten large piles of earth. American Indians built these more than 2,000 years ago. Adena and Hopewell people likely used them for religious purposes. Visitors can learn about the mounds by taking a tour.

Landmarks

Indiana is home to several landmarks. One is Cataract Falls, a beautiful series of waterfalls on Mill Creek in western Indiana. They are the state's largest waterfalls by volume. Nearby is Cagles Mill Lake Nature Center. There, people can learn how the falls formed.

Cataract Falls consists of two waterfalls. Visitors can view the falls from a historic covered bridge.

Visitors can also learn about the Miami, Shawnee, and Potawatomi peoples who once lived in the area.

Southwestern Indiana is home to the Lincoln Boyhood National Memorial. This is where Abraham Lincoln grew up. He was the sixteenth US president. When Lincoln was seven years old,

The Lincoln Boyhood National Memorial includes a living history farm. Actors in historical clothing teach visitors about life on the Lincoln family farm.

his family moved to Indiana from Kentucky. The cabin Lincoln lived in is no longer standing. But its location is marked for visitors.

Crossroads of America

Indiana's state motto is "The Crossroads of America." This is because Indianapolis lies at the intersection of several interstate highways. These include I-65, I-70, and I-465. People use these roads to transport goods and travel across the state and the country.

Indiana's state flag features 19 stars and a flaming torch.

In Indianapolis, people can visit the Indianapolis Zoo. They can see elephants, lions, snakes, and baboons. In Elkhart, people can visit the Wellfield Botanic Gardens. These contain 36 acres (15 ha) of plants and water.

Indiana contains a variety of landmarks, historical sites, and cultures. Visitors can watch race cars zoom by on the Indianapolis Motor Speedway. They can swim in Lake Michigan. They can visit historical sites and learn about the state's past. Everyone who passes through Indiana can find something there to fascinate them.

> ### Further Evidence
> Look at the website below. Does it give any new evidence to support Chapter Three?
>
> ### Indiana
> abdocorelibrary.com/discovering-indiana

State Map

Indianapolis

KEY
 Capital    Park
City or town   Point of interest

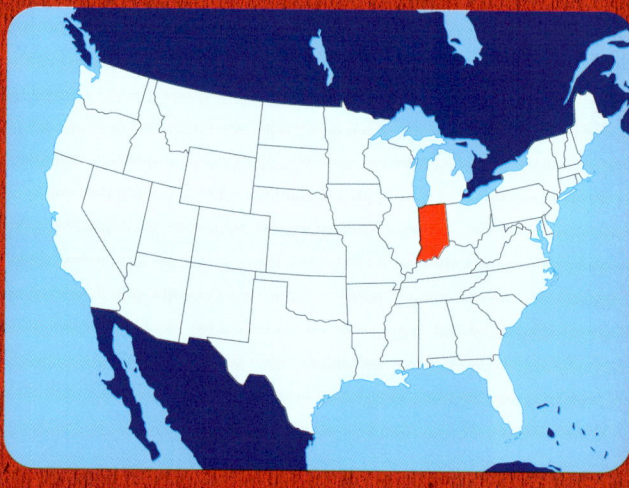

Indiana Dunes National Park

University of Notre Dame

28

Indiana: The Hoosier State

- Lake Michigan
- Michigan
- South Bend
- University of Notre Dame
- Indiana Dunes National Park
- Chain O'Lakes State Park
- Fort Wayne
- Wabash River
- Illinois
- Mounds State Park
- Indianapolis Motor Speedway
- Indianapolis
- Ohio
- Cataract Falls
- Monroe Lake
- Ohio River
- Wabash River
- Evansville
- Lincoln Boyhood National Memorial
- Kentucky

29

Glossary

acquired
came into possession of

colonists
people who have moved to and taken control of an area

fertile
able to produce healthy plant growth

immigrants
people who move to a different country

kettle lakes
lakes in holes formed by ice melting from glaciers

manufacturing
making goods to sell

territory
an area of land that belongs to someone

Online Resources

To learn more about Indiana, visit our free resource websites below.

Visit **abdocorelibrary.com** or scan this QR code for free Common Core resources for teachers and students, including vetted activities, multimedia, and booklinks, for deeper subject comprehension.

Visit **abdobooklinks.com** or scan this QR code for free additional online weblinks for further learning. These links are routinely monitored and updated to provide the most current information available.

Learn More

Abdo, Kenny. *Indianapolis Colts*. Abdo, 2022.

Indiana Dunes National Park Activity Book. Little Bison, 2021.

Murray, Julie. *Indiana*. Abdo, 2020.

Index

Cataract Falls, 23
Chain O'Lakes State Park, 22–23

Delaware nation, 14

farming, 9, 13, 18, 19
food, 15–16

Indiana Dunes National Park, 22
Indianapolis, 6, 7, 16–17, 21, 25, 26–27
Indianapolis 500, 5–7, 27

Lake Michigan, 7, 9, 11, 22, 27
Lincoln Boyhood National Memorial, 24–25

Miami nation, 14, 24
Mounds State Park, 23

Potawatomi nation, 14, 24
Purdue University, 18

sports, 16–17
state symbols, 6

University of Notre Dame, 18

About the Author

Ib Larsen is a writer and editorial assistant living in Saint Paul, Minnesota.